Hans Hammarskiöld

STOCKHOLM
The Four Seasons

Text by Niklas Rådström

Translated from Swedish by Joan Tate

Stockholm – Cultural Capital of Europe '98

Wahlström & Widstrand / Gedins

I

Autumn rain, flowing over metal roofs, squares and roadways, everywhere forming waterfalls and watercourses in drainpipes and gutters. For a few moments these narrow, coiling rivers are blocked by heaps of red, brown and yellow autumn leaves, then the water again breaks through and meanders down on to the pavement and on towards the drains of the crossroads.

Cars throw surges of rainwater up over the paving-stones, and pedestrians hurry along close to the walls, away from the violent downpour, forced to leap over the largest puddles in gutters like steeplechasers over a water jump, before escaping reasonably dry-shod indoors.

The high cliffs along the steep shore of Södermalm are blackened with moisture, and at the crossing, a squall of rain rushing down Götgatsbacken parts, some water apparently heading towards Lake Mälaren, the rest making its way across the paving-stones and asphalt to add to the brackish waters of Saltsjön.

Then the rain stops for a while, like a memory, leaving behind a miserly drizzle in the dusk. The small crowd sheltering in a porchway out of the downpour looks up at the grey clouds sweeping by. Someone holds out a hand, palm open to the sky, and establishes that the rain has retreated to reassemble its forces.

The ferry we take in the failing light of late afternoon from the island of Djurgården over to the steps at Räntmästartrappan is only half full — a class of tired school youngsters on their way home after a study day at Skansen, some pensioners who have spent an afternoon walking between the museums of Djurgården, and a pair of lovers with eyes for nothing in the city but each other.

Out on the after-deck is a grave man with a bushy beard and wet clothes. He could be taken for a vagrant, had it not been for the heavy coat of mail under his coat. The rain wets his dark, lined face, and drops of water glisten in his greying beard in the reflection from spotlights on

In the mid-thirteenth century, Birger Jarl was the Regent of Sweden.
Although Stockholm was already an expanding town, he is considered to
be its founder from when in the summer of 1252, together with his son
King Valdemar, he dates a letter in the town.

a building site in Skeppsholmen. He stands there sturdily, his feet wide apart on the deck — as if on legs used to rough seas and with a look that questions how he came to be on just this craft.

Autumn is the season when the city is renewed.

Some islets where Lake Mälaren meets Saltsjön, a fishing hamlet with a frail little cottage, small, open boats bobbing, fish scales shimmering on their boards, some hawsers in the water by rickety jetties, cliffs, forest, a herd of bleating goats… And this is where we build our city. A drop falls from an oar into the sea and in the rings on the water, the city can be seen growing: some houses, a tower… Rings on the water. Year rings. Rings of time. Seasons. Soon — it takes only a hundred years or so of seasons, year rings, rings on the water: a throng of buildings and streets. The city evolves in one single stroke of the oar.

Now that autumn ensures that the days grow darker earlier and earlier in the evening, the season of clearing sales begins, sales of all those left over requisites of summer — drifts of T-shirts and bathing costumes, garden furniture at firewood prices, remainders of what had been hoped would be the fashion for the summer. The book-shop windows display the new autumn titles, and the travel agencies are already marketing opportunities to escape from approaching darkness and cold.

In the autumn, the city empties of its casual visitors and the city dwellers can at last return from their summer places of exile, holidays and travels. They look after their houses, buy new furniture and scan the adverts for apartments. The return to the autumn city — where the heat of summer has squeezed the last life out of the house-plants placed out on balconies and in back courtyards — makes them want to make everything new, to start again from the beginning and have the old city seem new.

The man on the after-deck has sailed to the Bay of Bothnia and the Bay of Riga, exchanged his Chinese silk and Arabian silver in the trading places of the Black Sea, carried goods between the islands of Lake Mälaren, deep in among forest and rock. We can read about his friends on a rune-stone near Gripsholm Castle:

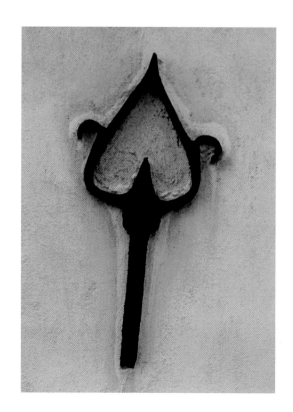

Boldly they voyaged
far away for gold
and in the east
fed the eagle.
Southwards
they died
in Saracen land.

Birger Jarl jerks open the cabin door on the Djurgården ferry and strides forcefully through the listless afternoon chatter of the school children. He brushes away their talk in the damp air inside the ferry, and by the time he has reached the door to the foredeck, they have all fallen silent. Someone asks whether the man is a mental patient escaped from the hospital's exercise yard and now day after day walking through the city, agitatedly talking to himself. But the man going through the warm damp interior of the ferry is the one who will in all times be regarded as the founder of Stockholm. The dark coat of mail under his coat seems stiff and rusty, and he moves like a statue to which the autumn has given life and mobility.

Autumn is an assiduous and conscientious bureaucrat: each and

every leaf is to be marked with his fiery yellow stamp before they are gathered into mounds of composting leaves in the parks. He goes there with his briefcase, shabby from darkness and time, misting over the window-panes with his fingers. Children, in waterproof trousers and rubber boots, clamber all over the heaps of leaves left behind him, like space-men exploring an unknown planet.

Autumn runs through the city, dallies at the shopwindows and looks into interiors of cafés, stopping by a ramshackle house near Stortorget, where he sees the amputated ears and plaits of punishments by mutilation. Adulterers must stand on the roof of the low house with their shame. Behind a hatch, the Moneylord, as the executioner is called, counts the coins given to him by the condemned for his trouble. He counts them just as carefully as autumn counts the yellowing leaves on the trees, the wilting grass in the park, the pearly drops in the curtain of rain.

The oldest Swedish interpretation of how Stockholm acquired its name is also the most beautiful: legend has it that the inhabitants of Sigtuna, after their town had been destroyed by the ravages of an Estonian raiding expedition, filled a log with gold and silver, pushed it out into the water and built a town on the holm where the log floated ashore.

Other tales are perhaps more likely, but less fantastic.

As Birger Jarl stands on the foredeck of the Djurgården ferry in his damp coat and greying beard, watching the ferry approaching the steps at Räntmästartrappan, naturally he knows that its place by the water has always been crucial to Stockholm. That has been clear to them all. Engelbrekt knows it in the autumn of 1434 when in a damp mean wind he besieges Långholmen, while the Sörmlanders settle on Åsön and the Upplanders on Norrmalm. Sten Sture knows it thirty-seven years later when with autumn sprays in their caps and helmets, his army advances on the Danish King Christian's forces at Brunkeberg.

Stockholm of the Middle Ages was one of the most important trading towns around the Baltic Sea, half German, sometimes in alliance and sometimes in conflict with Lübeck and the Hanseatic League. One of the strong men of the fourteenth century, Bo Jonsson, in one single year exported more than 8,000 pounds of wax and 29,000 pelts, 11,000 of them ermine. The town was periodically dominated by the Vitale brothers — plunderers and pirates who made raids all over the Bay of Bothnia, even going as far as kidnapping the Bishop of Strängnäs and throwing him into Stockholm's prison tower.

Two hundred years later, at the end of the sixteenth century, the town was neither dominated by trade nor piracy. Of the almost twelve hundred breadwinners, two thirds were in the service of the King. On the main island were 743 houses, while on the other islands they had their livestock, small patches of land, and sheds behind the fences of the holdings. A French visitor in the 1630s complains about the houses of the nobility being no better than the cottages the simplest Parisian merchant had built for himself. Tapestries are rare among Stockholm's nobility. The only ornament in the main room being a blue ceiling-hanging above the table so that the spiders shall not fall into the food.

Now the shutters are being closed in the town alleyways against the autumn damp. But nonetheless the damp penetrates everywhere, however much the fires are stoked. Between the walls, other things often fall, apart from rain. St Bridget demonstrated her gentleness when she gave nothing but a pious reply to one of her enemies who sent a shower of dirty water over her as she walked along one of the alleyways.

In Österlånggatan the replica of the statue of St George and the Dragon, in its eternal single combat, is longing to change places with the

Storkyrkan (the Great Church),
Gamla Stan (the Old Town)

13

original in the warmth of Storkyrkan (the Great Church). Sten Sture commissioned this sculptural group to celebrate the memory of the Battle of Brunkeberg that had been fought on St George's Day, October 10th, 1471. A yearly procession used to be held on that day, bringing the host, censers and reliquaries to the battlefield outside the city.

The Djurgården ferry shudders as it hits the edge of the quay at the Räntmästartrappan. The school children have already dispersed and are standing round the man out on the foredeck, pleased to be back home soon. When the gates open, they pour past the dark figure in his damp coat. He is still hesitating over whether to go ashore. It is late afternoon in Stockholm. Autumn. A gentle rain is falling.

The other passengers walk past the large man, who is finally left there alone. The ferry conductor wonders whether there is going to be trouble. But then the man takes a stride over towards the quay, swaying like an old seaman, dizzy once there is firm ground beneath his feet. The heavy, double-bladed sword he has under his coat scrapes against the edge of the quay as he steps ashore. He stands there holding on to the upright of the traffic lights by the pedestrian crossing, like a drunk going ashore from the Finland ferry.

In the drizzle, a half-open car drives past. The woman in the back behind the driver has turned up her collar against the draught. The man by the crossing meets her eyes for a moment. He has just arrived in a city that does not yet exist, and she is about to leave for a life under a new name in a country of dreams. Film director Mauritz Stiller awaits her. The labels on her suitcases, already packed for her departure on the ship to America, have for several years borne her new name: Greta Garbo. The man on the crossing watches the car and tries to remember where he has seen her before.

A namesake of his, Birger Brosa, God only knows how many years ago, built a granite defence tower on the highest point of the island at Norrström. But the dark figure, that the increasing rain now appears to be enveloping in its damp veils, is going to make this city his. As soon as the traffic lights change, Birger Jarl is to cross the road and go on to found the city that is to be given the name Stockholm.

Old wooden houses on Södermalm

Morning walk in Kronoberg park

Stretching i Humlegården

Whortleberry trade in
Hötorget (the Haymarket)

Outside the Royal Palace

In Klara district

Vasastaden and Gustaf Vasa Church ▷

"The Archer" on Observatory Hill

The City Library in Sveavägen.

The Brunkeberg's tunnel between Sveavägen and Birger Jarlsgatan is a subterranean shortcut open to the public. Beneath the surface of the city lies a whole town of winding tunnels for drainage and water, electricity and telecommunications. The shops have underground goods receptions, and the Parliament building is connected with Government offices through elaborate tunnels.

II

AT NIGHT, the winter snow seems to enclose the city in a sphere similar to the souvenirs that innumerable tourists take with them home from their travels to foreign cities. Shake the sphere for a moment and the snow suddenly swirls up from the pavement round some familiar area or building.

Harsh winters again freeze the watercourses and lakes round the city. The boats lie frozen in, if not drawn up ashore for overhaul during the winter. A tourist visiting Stockholm at the end of the sixteenth century is amazed at how the city's women are carried on sleighs, ladies are borne like infants in cradles, covered right up to their faces by the furs bound round them. There is nothing they can do if the sledge tips over or the horses bolt, for they are totally dependent on the skill of the driver standing behind the sleigh. The visitor also complains about the lack of entertainment in the winter.

But a coffee-house is open for an early porridge breakfast, the moist warmth in the café misting over the windows facing the street. At the bus stop outside is a morning-weary crowd on its way to work, the day hardly dawned. The darkness of night seems to have set into the day like grease and dirt in an old dishcloth. But a squally wind, that makes the snow howl round the corners, slowly squeezes life into the traffic, and a pale sky begins to glimpse above the glow of the street lights.

Inside the café, someone bends down and plugs in the old pinball machine in the corner of the room. A little bell lets out a delicate clang from inside the machine, and the calculator spins and stops at nought. A loud click can be heard as the coin rolls down through the slot in the side and a gleaming silvery steel ball rolls out into the track. Outside, a bus at last stops by the post and picks up the frozen horde out there. It gradually becomes light over the city, the clouds flee one by one, and the sky turns bright blue and high. Clouds billow out of the mouths of passers-by and the cars slither on the carriageways.

Sofia Church and the Globe

Winter is the season when the city is renewed.

As the autumn has been taken unawares by the first snowfall of the winter, everything is different. Cars skid into ditches along approach roads into the city. Pedestrians slide around as if snow were not a natural part of the changing seasons, but a sudden attack of another dimension from outer space. Everything that was dark and damp yesterday, is now in the morning ironed newly white.

The habits of everyday dissolve. The city's familiar map, its streets and crossings, is at once wiped out and the map has turned dazzlingly white. Motorists, who usually rage at each other at far too bold lane changes, slide round like silver balls in the café's pinball machine. The drivers appear to have never heard of either lanes or pavements.

Just as new paths are always appearing alongside the gravel pathways in parks in the summer, city motorists create their own traffic reorganisation after the first snowfall of winter. Astonished, the citizens go out into their new white city as if into totally foreign territory.

City dwellers are what the writer Frans G. Bengtsson calls "all central heating people". They complain about the inconveniences of winter:

> *Trains don't arrive, travel plans fall apart, perhaps there's no milk for breakfast, the entire image of the world is thrown out of gear; because somewhere, winter has coughed carelessly on the tracks where communications run by the clock, or has spat into sad time-table people's most ingenious signal-box arrangements.*

In contrast to country people's sturdier relations to snow and cold, the central heating person turns to the landlord and complains: "It's too cold!"

In town, only the churchyards' conifers escape being drawn into the confusion of winter and continue in their calm:

> *"It's cold," mumble the pines, "but we stay green; but we endure — throughout our time."*

When the library opens at Medborgarplatsen, several figures are already huddled in the doorway. Slowly their joints thaw out in the newspaper reading-room. A man with matted shoulder-length hair and a greasy beard sits in his chair with the winter ice of a whole night melting into a

Bastugatan, Södermalm

faintly intimated damp patch round him. He is talking quietly to himself, reading page after page of an old financial paper. The lack of topicality in the stock exchange news is not his problem. A mild smell of damp wool and rags spreads as the night chill in the warmth of the room relinquishes its hold on his clothes.

In another library in another part of the city is another man. He is wondering what he is doing there, sitting at a desk in the old Castle, cursing at the Nordic cold. It was still autumn when he came to Stockholm a few months earlier. Flights of birds rose over the water and the autumn was slowly colouring the trees in Ladugårdslandet yellow and red. But winter has now taken its hold on the city. René Descartes is dissatisfied with the food, imprisoned in the cold and coughing like a mangey dog.

He has been corresponding for several years with Queen Kristina and has finally received a royal invitation to come to Stockholm. The Queen of Sweden has stated that she wishes to understand his philosophy, but hitherto nothing much has been said. He has made a few barometer measurements on behalf of Pascal, and he has been asked to compose a ballet, assisted by a rather over-tense lawyer by the name of Stiernhjelm in writing the Swedish text. Finally he has wasted several weeks writing a comedy. The thought that his countrymen would laugh more loudly at his French scenes warms him in his loneliness in this icy northern cold.

It is cold in the Royal Library and some of the books bulge with damp. Descartes coughs, nevertheless perhaps likes the noise he makes, for his cough sounds the same as it did in the streets of Paris and that gives him a feeling of being at home despite everything. As he gazes out of the window at the ice on the waters round the Castle, at the rays of the sun sparkling in ice crystals and the sleighs racing over the frozen waters of Strömmen, snow swirling round their runners, he thinks that the snow of northern winter after all mocks the darkness of northern winter. As an increasingly large part of the day ends in obscurity and shadows, winter deceives the darkness by painting the landscape white.

But perhaps this French philosopher has simply had a bad day. Candles and oil lamp wicks are lit in room after room in the district. A lamplighter is already starting out on his round through the city,

The state coach is used when foreign envoys are presented at Court.

and in another district and in another century, neon lights hiss and wink. The last gaslighting gleamed in Stockholm's streets as recently as 1941, and today no place in the city lies in complete darkness.

Someone cuts across the frozen Riddarfjärden on a bicycle. A team of workers is on its way with ice-saws to keep a channel open. With a warmer season in mind, they have marsh-sledges with them to take ice back to the townspeople's cellars and ice-stacks. Through the inn window in a dark area, the falling snow glows in a warm light. A group of men have been sitting inside since early on in the day and a waitress has slipped over to the bar to get a drink for herself. Icicles and small avalanches of snow slide off the roofs. A man in a fur hat and black coat asks pedestrians to stop while his colleague hammers free an icicle several metres long from the gutter five floors up. In a snug inn in Österlånggatan, a table for regulars has been laid.

In Vita Berget park, toboggans race hither and thither down the slopes, and in Humlegården there is a snowman, his features slowly melting, the two drooping branches for arms in an increasingly collapsing embrace. In Vanadislunden, some snowboard riders have built a ramp from which they jump and crouch. Some kindergarten children watch in awe. In 1889, an international figure skating competition was arranged on the ice in Nybroviken. A platform for the judges was constructed on one of the quays. Flags and pennants were hoisted and from the windows of one of the new apartment blocks along Strandvägen, a recently married couple stood watching. The man ran his hand over his wife's swollen stomach. Their first child was to be born that spring.

Outside the department store in Hamngatan, families walk slowly past, gazing in at the Christmas decorations. In the great store windows, mechanical dolls move in stiff poses, as if they were the last remaining actors from the variety show once housed in the seventeenth century palace that had previously been on the site. From a baker's store in Gamla Stan (the Old Town), en empty bread-sledge is hauled back to the bakery in Södermalm. The sledge is used all the year round, but now during the winter it has been given iron-clad runners.

The French philosopher has departed from the library, leaving the book he had been reading still open on the desk. He is now standing out on Slottsbacken, despite his cough and far too thin shoes. Below the old Castle, tall stacks of firewood stand on Skeppsbron, and frozen in by the quay

Outer courtyard of the Royal Palace

are two small cargo boats, their masts bare and hatches battened down. They remind him of coffins that cannot be put into the earth as long as the frost maintains its hold on the ground.

René Descartes walks towards Storkyrkan, its high gable rising to the skies, where a streak of gold from the fleeing sun momentarily breaks through the clouds. Descartes has always regarded the solar fire material, as a fine and fleeting subject out of which the sun and all the stars have assembled. In a few decades, a bishop's son by the name of Emanuel Swedenborg is to be tempted by the same gold dust. Sun material has been developed to such a fine degree, he is to think, that it is home to God and the angels and all those things that have nothing material in their nature.

Swedenborg. While Cartesius wanders down towards Strömmen to make his way over to the north island, Emanuel Swedenborg goes out on to the wintry yard outside his property in the Mullvaden (Mole) district. For a moment, he thinks he glimpses a faint light in the pavilion further down the garden. He thinks that it must be cold in there, but the spirits presumably do not freeze in earthly cold. A dream has been following him since the morning and he cannot decide whether he should interpret it as a reproach from God or simply as a request. In the newly fallen snow, he can see a series of footprints. Perhaps a labourer has passed by, or maybe one of those inquisitive people who otherwise come to look

Storkyrkan (the Great Church)
and the Royal Palace

at his garden and pavilion in the summer. Or are they the footprints of the angel who sat at his bedside while he was dreaming?

When René Descartes is half way across Norrbro (the North Bridge), he has become one of the city's angels. He is already dead. His cough simply grew worse and his breathing more laboured with every day that passed, until finally his fever conquered the Swedish winter and his body no longer froze. But by then his breath was as short as prepositions, all meaning had disappeared from his language and when he ceased breathing, all was silent. René Descartes remained in Stockholm, and as he wanders across Norrbro, not only he, but also the Queen is dead. A handful of regents have already sat on her throne. The present King is this evening holding a masquerade at the Royal Opera at the north end of the bridge.

When Cartesius turns round on the bridge, he finds that the old Castle with its dark towers is no longer there. Instead there is a new Palace, a huge creation with a flat roof and tall windows. He sees lamplight in some of the rooms, and in others, shadows at a ball. He goes on northwards across the bridge and finally stops to gaze at the lights in the windows of the Royal Opera House. There he stays, a vanishing shadow in the falling snow.

Just as we pass the place where he is standing, we hear the music from the Opera House. Stop, halt the traffic and listen. Of course they are playing music? Perhaps it is a ballet being performed, perhaps an opera, or is it a masquerade? And then… Before we have had time to think the thought through, a sudden shot is heard. A figure in a dark coat hurtles out of a side door, runs towards a waiting carriage and just as the light changes on the pedestrian crossing, someone cries out from inside that

the King has been shot. It is snowing and the wounded monarch, King Gustav III, is borne in a carriage across Norrbro to the Palace. The snow falls and almost two centuries later another shot is heard and a pavement in Sveavägen is coloured a blood-spattered red.

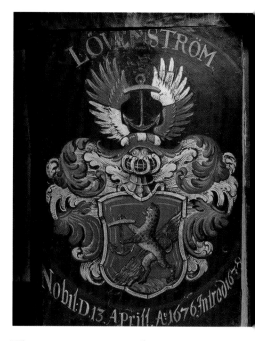

The assassination of King Gustav III at a masked ball in the winter of 1792 marked the end of an epoch in the history of Sweden. The coat of arms of the assassin, Anckarström, in Riddarhuset (the House of Nobility) was repainted after the sentence to suit the new family name, Löwenström.

Department of Foreign Affair

*Celebrators of Lucia Day,
December 13th, in Östermalms-
torg underground station*

Old wooden buildings on Skinnarviksberget, Södermalm

The Royal Skating Association used
this beautiful building as its club-
house from 1882 to 1901, when King
Oscar II lost interest in skating. It is
said that as long as the flag flies above
Kastellet (the Citadel), Sweden will
live in peace.

Nybroviken ▷

*In the 1890s, at Skansen in Djurgården, Artur Hazelius created an
open-air museum as a Sweden-in-miniature with a wealth of examples
of the flora, fauna and cultural history of the country.*

◁ *The af Chapman Youth Hostel, Skeppsholmen*

On cold winter days Stock-holmers stroll or skate on the ice of Riddarfjärden.

View of Gamla Stan (the Old Town) from Stadsgården ▷

56

Model in Stadsmuseet (the City Museum) of the old Tre Kronor (Three Crowns) Castle

THE ICY SLUSH of winter is still racing along with Strömmen's spring flood on May 7th 1697, when a few sparks, perhaps from the palace workers' canteen in the attic, set fire to the inside of the tinder-dry flooring, and the entire Castle is rapidly enveloped in flames. The coffin containing the recently deceased King Karl XI is hastily removed to safety. When the fire breaks out, it is a bright spring afternoon, sunny, with clear sky.

For several years, plans have been nourished for a new and more modern Palace, but if the fire had not broken out, perhaps none of them would have materialized. Or then, as someone had suggested, a new Palace would have been built in Södermalm next to Katarina Church's stately cupola. Then maybe a different parish from Katarina would have been the poorest in Stockholm over the centuries.

Stockholm's frozen winter people have always dreamt of their city as bright and filled with the summer season's warmth. In the seventeenth century, Governor Rosenhane imagines a Garden of Eden out at Kungsholmen. There vines, apricots and peaches, hazel-nuts, currants, and gooseberries were to grow behind the fences. Some decades later, a doctor by the name of Hallman hit on the idea of breeding silkworms, and therefore planted 25,000 mulberry trees in a garden out in Ladugårdslandet. However, no silkworms had time to spin their threads before winter eventually clasped the trees in its cold arms and bowed them to the ground.

In the allotments at Tanto, on the slope below the Sachska Children's Hospital, the plots are already newly dug. A dreamer might perhaps take the roar from the Essinge road morning traffic to be a spring flood. Seed potatoes and plants, seeds and bulbs for autumn flowers are collected in a basket. The allotment holder carefully plans his rows for sowing, the damp soil thickly caked on his dark green rubber boots. He has stretched white cotton ribbon across the dark earth between sticks at the sides of the plot and on the bench by the little allotment shack are a thermos of coffee and a box of sandwiches.

Carl von Linné, Linneaus the Botanist, who once had an apartment in Räntmästarhuset by Slussen that was later taken over by the twenty years older Swedenborg, is at every allotment grower's side during the spring sowing. He looks at plants, seed packets, and cuttings and whispers Latin names into the grower's ear. The grower listens and dreams of his summer vegetable plot and autumn harvest of asters, but he does not let the old man's mumble interrupt his work. In the end, Linné grows tired and sits down next to the thermos flask on the bench. He sits quite still, just nodding slightly when the seeds are at last in the soil. Spring, someone has said, is the cradle of the entire year.

Spring is the season of miracles and ecstasy. In the old days, it says in the collected miracles of the Dominican monastery, a man who had gone mad during a bear hunt was saved from his madness by the message of spring. A fatally sick horse was cured, a lost boy found, ships saved from terrible storms, condemned innocents found grace and freedom. Today the magazine placards are filled with slimming tips and health cures. All the rubbish and mustiness of winter is to be chased out of bodies with intense and merciless exorcism, in the hope that we shall be able to face the summer with new bodies.

On a balcony in Vasastaden, a small greenhouse has been constructed, inside it the tomato plants already beginning to shoot. At the top of the building, a window is thrown open and an attic store-room is being cleaned out and aired. A young man pushes up a hatch in a metal roof on the other side of the courtyard, climbs up to the roof-ridge and sits there with a newspaper and a can of beer. But the newspaper cannot distract his interest in the view before his eyes. The whole city lies at the young man's feet, roof-ridge after roof-ridge, a frozen sea of metal. On the tops of chimneys, like an attentive tennis audience, dark ballerinas move as the spring gusts serve and respond with surprising returns. And then — high above the roof top, a multi-coloured balloon comes floating, the burner hissing below the balloon opening, the passengers leaning over the edge of the basket, staring down at the city like angels out sightseeing.

Spring is the season when the city is renewed.

Streets are crowded in the middle of the day. You have to push your way between pedestrians who have gone out for their lunch hour. The crush is perhaps as great as during one of the seven times the chief of the firebrigade

Globen (the Globe), Stockholm's great arena for events, and the rebuilt Katarina Church after the 1990 fire

had to run the gauntlets for dereliction of duty during the Castle fire, instead of the death sentence that he was first condemned to. On the racks of hanging blouses on the pavements, the wind and passers-by take it in turns to grab at the remains of last year's range, now being sold off.

On the steps of Konserthuset (the Concert Hall), banks of people sit warming themselves in the rays of the spring sun, bags of fruit and lunch bought in Hötorget between them, garments being removed one after another. Winter-pallid shoulders and arms are warmed in the sunshine. Some solaria-brown fitness freaks can at last display the bunched muscles they have been working on all winter in some basement premises. Previously, farmers from the county of Uppland came here to the Hötorget (the Haymarket) to pay their taxes in hay for fodder for the horses in the royal stables.

Once the steets on Brunkeberg ridge were steep and winding, wooden buildings climbing along crooked roads over the slopes, until one spring day in 1640 when the thatched roofs and wall insulation caught fire on the east side of the ridge. Several hundred holdings were burnt to the ground, and the homeless were given new land in Ladugårdslandet, which the Crown had just donated to the city. Just as the spring grower on his allotment marks out his furrows with white cotton string over all that has decayed in the soil, so a new city plan is marked out in the ash after the fire, the streets straight like in renaissance Italy. The street-plan of east Norrmalm is largely the same today.

At the same pace as the city extended out over the islands, team after team of rock-blasters, women sand-movers, dayworkers and excavators conquered the hills of Brunkebergsåsen. Huge quantities of gravel, load by load, have filled in marshes and wetlands, or formed new land along the shores. The lonely fisherman who once inhabited the main island notes the stem of his boat striking land in Lake Klara earlier and earlier for each year. A drop of water falls from his oar and the town expands like the rings in the water — the year rings, the rings of time, the seasons.

A few decades ago, the city planners and councillors finally transformed Brunkeberg ridge into a deep crater, as if it had been struck by a meteor. Deep down in the mud, bones of humans and animals were found, stone laid upon stone, layer after layer of street dirt and decayed waste, cracked herring barrels and decomposed taffeta. A sixteenth century palace stood perched upon the edge of a deep ravine, staring

The Observatory at Brunkeberg ridge was designed in the eighteenth century by the architect Carl Hårleman.

down into the abyss. Later a new town grew out of there, a town that had forgotten the stroller's need for corners to turn, for alleys to take refuge in during sudden spring showers, lines following the city's own nature more than those of the drawing-board. But Stockholmers have also made this new town their own.

A window is open four floors up in Drottninggatan. The man renting the place perhaps already knows this is the last address of his life. The winter has been icy cold and the spring warmth, the lofty skies where the light slowly is taking flight, the swallows high up above the metal roofs, the sound of people walking in the streets, horses' hooves and the occasional motor-car – all have a wonderful lightness.

A week or two ago, Walpurgis bonfires were burning all round the waters of the city. Then he had yearned for his Djurgår-den, but he had stayed in the north island. In the old days, a beacon was lit at Nämdö when the enemy's sails hove into sight on the horizon, and soon one bonfire after another passed on the message of danger approaching far into the inner archipelago. Now the bonfires bring the message of the invasion of spring.

In 1908, August Strindberg moved to his final residence, Blå Tornet (the Blue Tower) in Drottninggatan 85. By then he had had about twenty-five addresses in town. His last residence is now a museum and his initials can be seen on the façade of the building.

How many times has he not left this city only to return each time? A few years ago he wrote about the transformation of the city when a new plan sought to realize an esplanade system on the Parisian model. He wondered whether perhaps it was not enough to demolish here for light and air. But sometimes he might ask asked himself whether the new stone city with its high façades did not shut the light out from the streets down there. Are the pavements not more often in the shade nowadays, or is it that his eyes have grown dimmer?

Anyhow, the spring light does reach the tower in Drottninggatan where he lives. The trees flourish round the Observatory on the hill. In the sky, flight after flight of birds race by. If he were not so tired, and if he could for once occasionally escape the grinding pain in his stomach, then he would go out. He contents himself with leaving the window open, although spring has not really had time to decorate his winter home. But it is growing lighter, if only slowly, growing as light as the spring can manage.

Down in the small boatyards in Lake Mälaren, boats have been launched over the weekend. A bunch of newly varnished boats lie in Slussen waiting for the water to sink to the level of Saltsjön. With frozen fingers in the spring sun, which has not yet entirely warmed them, crews stay in their craft at the quays. The first lock built here was completed in 1642 and was named after Queen Kristina. A hundred years later, Christoffer Polhem constructed a new lock that was called Röda Slussen (the Red Lock) after the colour of the four towers decorating the west lock bridge. On the Saltsjö side, the lock was named after the towers which there were blue. The present Slussen is an extension of the one constructed by Nils Ericson in the mid-nineteenth century.

In Humlegården, dams and watercourses are also being built, though these are intended only for sticks and paper-boats of children kneeling in their waterproof trousers, small plastic spades in their hands. Round the plinth of the Carl von Linné statue, all the water that runs through the delta on the slope from Karlavägen collects and turns into the Seven Seas. A boy has discovered that what is left of the autumn's half-dead leaves strengthens his dam and he shovels more and more on. But the spring flood breaks through all the same, and winds its way towards open water. The imaginary dam-builder is drawn with it into the racing water – a toy car is in the way and is wash-

Carl von Linné (Linneaus the Botanist) is one of the most famous Swedes of all time. This is one of the saddles on which he might have been seen riding from Uppsala to be present at a meeting of the Royal Swedish Academy of Sciences in Riddarhuset (the House of Nobility).

ed over by the mass of water. A small dream figure manages to escape via a narrow branch protruding out over the raging currents. This is a natural disaster of such magnitude, not even the cries of the play leaders to come for refreshments manages to stop it.

Strindberg rents the three rooms, four floors up, from the parents of a girl he has found as a supernumerary at the Intima Teatern. He wanted

Norr Mälarstrand is the most fashionable street in Kungsholmen. The houses with the stepped gables, crowned with statues, were built in the 1920s.

Fanny Falkner, as she is called, for the title role in his play Swanwhite. When she goes to see him, he treats her with avuncular warmth and has scarcely the energy left to yearn to be seduced yet again. He thinks she has infinite talent for theatre, but she does not really trust his word.

To be left in peace, he has written a short list of rules to his host family, on it instructions that he is not to be disturbed by unimportant errands, and no stranger is to be let unannounced into his room. Finally, he has added that if his hall door is bolted, then that is not to be taken that he is "angry", but just a sign that he does not wish to be disturbed.

Karlaplan, Östermalm

But today, as the spring air fills the city, he would receive any unimportant errand with delight, and any stranger would arouse his curiosity. But most of all, he wishes Fanny would come. He hardly has time to think that thought through when he hears the door into the stairway opening. She comes to him with his evening meal now dusk has fallen outside. They have been playing at being an engaged couple for a week or two, but perhaps it was no more than a game. She runs her hand over his forehead, the young girl, and lets her fingers play for a moment in his hair.

"Herr Strindberg," she says. "Let me close the window. There's a draught."

But he stops her. He asks her to wait a while. He tells her that it is spring, after all.

The trees in the parks are still holding their breath, not daring to trust the spring entirely. When spring floods flowed below Södermalm's hills, the water collected in marshes and swamps. It could be so wet in the houses that the water came over thresholds in the rooms. Round the house corners, small streams of meltwater ripple and the pavements are dusty after all the winter attempts to conquer the icy paths with sand.

Flora's Hill in Humlegården

The city has discovered its own spring sport, gutterball. The young stand there after school, seven paving-stones from the gutter crossing the pavement from the drainpipe on the façade. A hard little ball is thrown against the gutter, and the person who scores a hit gets the ball and is awarded a point. The re-laying of the city's pavements has meant that the game has died out. Today, when in icy winds we hardly dare

call spring by that name, we will surely find other evidence that winter is over. Not even that the fact that the football season has cautiously replaced the winter ice-hockey season manages to calm us down.

King Erik XIV's love of ball games could be trying for Stockholmers. They probably tolerated Bollhuset (the "Ball-house"), but it aroused strong feelings when he had courts made for his favourite sport shuttlecock, a mixture between badminton and tennis, on the churchyard graves. He thought the sport so important that he had a German ballmaker installed at Court.

We parents assemble during the boys' match beside a dusty suburban playing field, plastic mugs in our hands round the coffee thermos and the bag of buns, complaining about the referee like everyone else. The chalk marks are blowing all over the place in sudden gusts of spring, and a tearful child has to be helped off the field after colliding with an opponent. And so, in a cross-pass, a sudden rush towards goal or a bold breakaway, we are persuaded that the future contains nothing but opportunities.

In the window four floors up in Drottninggatan, Strindberg is at last on his own. He hears the piano being played on the floor above. The sky above the city is fiery red, blue and pink. He goes out on to his balcony, where he had stood for a moment in midwinter as a torchlight procession greeted him on the evening of his sixtieth birthday. Some of the cold of that winter evening remains in the air, but the spring wind does everything to tear it to shreds with its restless fingers. Then he is frightened by a sudden hissing above him. He looks up and sees the hot-air balloon drifting across the city and quietly gliding past just above the roof tops. the passengers staring down at him with the same astonishment with which he is staring up at them.

And you yourself have been standing at a window in another part of the city. You look out over the park and suddenly everything out there seems to have turned white. Has the cold not yet given up? But just as you think that despite everything you have not escaped winter, someone says:

"No, that's only the chestnut petals blowing off the trees."

Dragoons of the Life Guards on their way to
the changing of the guard

Functional architecture in Askrikegatan, Gärdet

Kaknäs Tower, Norra Djurgården

Hot-air balloons over City — a common sight on summer evenings

Strandvägen was planned in the 1860s, but the first houses were not built until in the early 1880s. This magnificent stretch was almost finished by the time of the Stockholm Exhibition in 1897, and has since been a popular promenade out to Djurgården.

King Karl XIV Johan had Rosendal's Palace built as he wanted a place to
have breakfast after the parades at Gärdet. Today this royal kitchen
garden, with its orchard and greenhouses, is a popular picnic ground. The
Palace's Empire style interior is one of the most well-preserved in Sweden.
This urn was carved in one single piece from a porphyry block of 1,000 tons
in Älvdalen. The finished urn, which has a weight of 9.3 tonnes, was
dragged to Stockholm by 175 men from Dalecarlia (Dalarna).

IV

THEN ONE DAY, spring with its chestnut petals has given up hesitating and summer is there, the air trembling above the hot asphalt. A boy on roller-skates races along the pavement, his bright red helmet bobbing between pedestrians. Those who a month or two ago were seeking out the sun wherever it had managed to break through, are now looking for a café table in the shade and are complaining about the heat.

Some children have crawled up on to the warm bronze lion in Kungsträdgården. Along the great esplanades, façades of buildings seem to crouch behind the shady greenery of the avenues. At the ice-cream kiosk at the north end of Djurgården bridge, a queue winds its way along the railing. Some kayaks and their sweating canoeists pause for a moment in the dimness and cool under the bridge. In one of the offices at Norra Bantorget, the accountant clerks have taken off their shoes. There is a faint splashing as a woman, who has put her feet into a bucket of cold water to cool herself, tries to beat time to music from a transistor radio.

Summer is the season when the city is renewed.

On a day like this in 1561, King Erik XIV enters the city, with ten trumpeters ahead of him, then behind the monarch innumerable hordes of bodyguards and lackeys, pages and courtiers – all in all a retinue of 310 horses. The King's horse is dazzling white with feathers on its head and tail. The streets have been swept and strewn with grass, walls and windows are covered with leafy branches and flags. Strings of woven flowers are suspended between the buildings, and everywhere there is the sound of strings and flutes, bassoons and French horns.

This evening, music will be coming from a large stage on the other side, the coloured lights from the spotlights winking in the water. Tents have been erected along the quays and long tables set up. The queues wind their way between stalls and toilets. You can have your fortune told here, or buy a T-shirt, on it the emblem of your favourite football team. You can buy a pike-skin tie, or a unique hand-painted

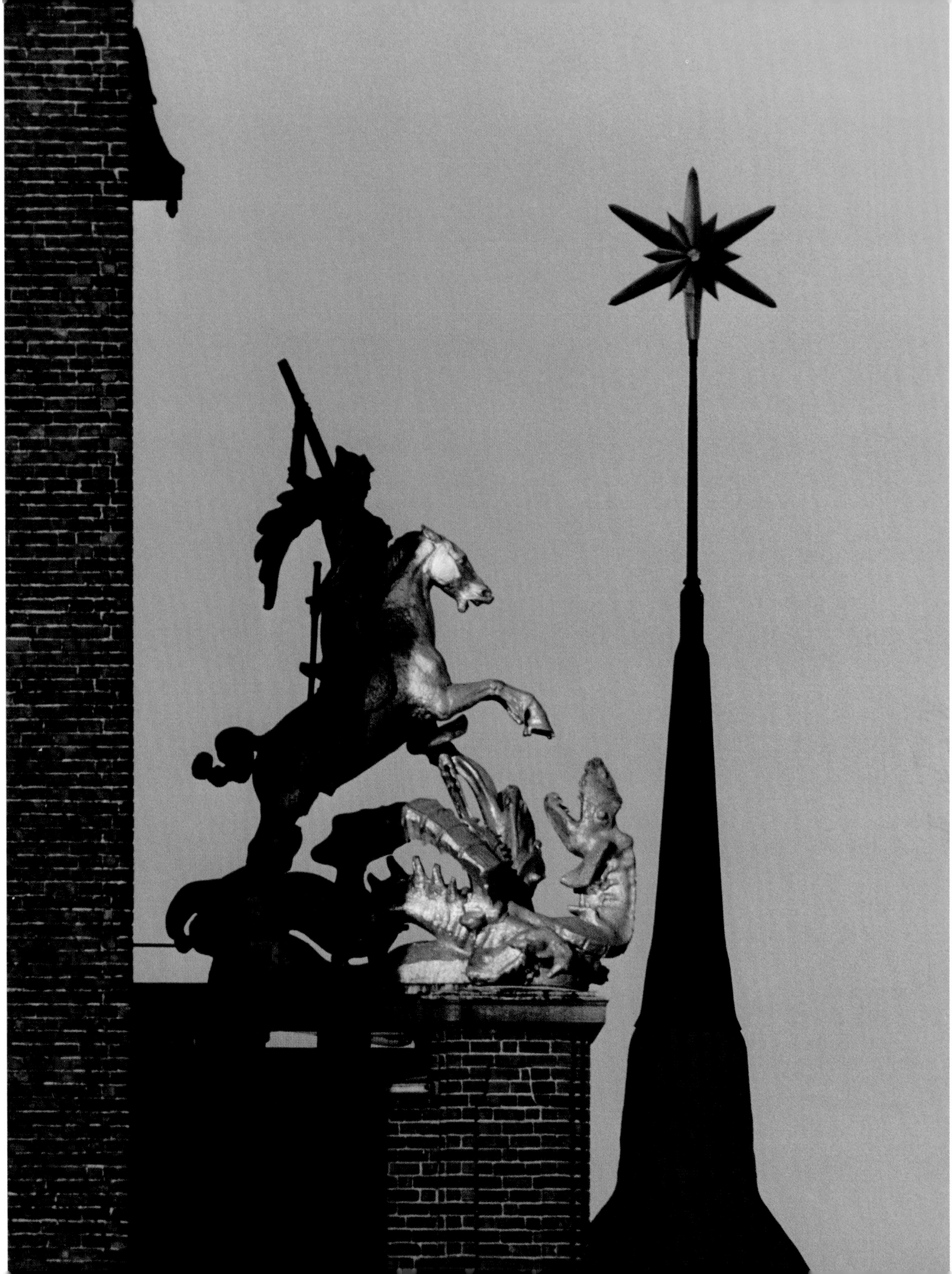

work of art can be yours. The smell of grilling mixes with the thumping rhythm from the stage, and at the tables plastic mugs of beer are raised. Look, the comedians have come to town!

We walk through Kungsträdgården – once the royal kitchen garden which Queen Kristina's French head gardener turned into a park of avenues and boxwood hedges. During the second half of the eighteenth century, the gates were opened to the public and on summer evenings, concerts, balls, and masquerades were arranged. Between ponds and orangeries, masked partygoers revelled and late at night, a statue stepped down from its plinth and joined in the dancing with a group of young people.

On the next site was the De la Gardie family's palace, Makalös (Matchless), one of the most imposing houses in town. Its hundreds of windows reflected the rays of the sun over the swirling waters of Strömmen, just like the revolving sphere today sends its glittering reflections over the couples on a dance floor. Makalös soon became an arsenal and after that a home for the Royal Minor Theatre. When the theatre caught fire during a performance in 1825, the walls round Kungsträdgården had already been pulled down, and the site of the fire became an empty space for military exercise. But in the shade of the avenues on the edges of this desert, social and café life continued and the greenery slowly spread again round the statue of King Karl XII and Molin's fountain.

Some Armenian merchants can be found there, come to town with a large consignment of Persian silk. Someone on a rug is selling clockwork reptiles of an Asian make. The mechanical plastic creatures crawl across the paving-stones towards the feet of passers-by. Over there some farmers from the county of Hälsingland have come to town with birchbark handicraft and hides, and in a narrow passage beneath the high gable of Jakob's Church, unmentionable things are being sold to restless customers with lost eyes and shaking limbs.

At Stockholm's 700 year anniversary in 1953, Kungsträdgården became a festive place in the centre of town and since then Stockholmers have looked on it as their own. Many inner city children have made their first attempts at skating on the artificial ice. When busybody city planners wanted to cut down the tall elms by the statue of King Karl XII, Stockholmers physically defended their garden, and the planned underground station had to be situated outside the park.

Stockholm's patron saint Sankt Göran (St George) not only slays the dragon in Storkyrkan (the Great Church) and in Österlånggatan, but also on the roof of Stadshuset (the City Hall).

The chimneys of Riddarhuset (the House of Nobility) appear to wish to remind us of Sweden's martial history by being designed as exploding shells. However, lighting fires in the fireplaces and tiled stoves of the building ceased long ago.

Dancing chimney ballerina in Högbergsgatan

Makalös (Matchless), the show palace of the de la Gardie family has today moved under-ground, where casts of the façade sculptures from the old building now ornament Kungs-trädgården underground station.

Lars Magnus Ericsson was one of the Swedish industrial geniuses
whose business enterprises are still known all over the world by their
names — Alfred Nobel, Gustaf de Laval, Gustaf Dalén… This tele-
phoning cherub hangs in the Ericsson memorial room that has been
moved from the old factory address, Tulegatan 17, and can now be
found in the Tekniska museet (the Museum of Technology).

At the bathing-place at Långholmen, shrieking children throw themselves into the water. It is hard to imagine that a few decades ago these waters were severely polluted. Raising the land and haphazard filling had over the years turned the shores into marshes out of which rose the stench of decay. The tanneries of Kungsholmen ruined Riddarfjärden, and the waters of Lake Klara were a muddy swamp.

All over town were dunghills and rubbish tips. Down at Kornhamnen (the Grain Harbour), so many flies gathered round the tips that the place was called the Fly-meeting. It was said that if the innumerable blue-green insects living there were ever disturbed, their buzzing swarms darkened the sun. However, this did not stop the homeless from creeping down into the horse manure to find a little warmth in winter.

Nybroviken once extended right into what is now Norrmalmstorg and gave rise to a number of epidemics when the heat of summer fermented the swampy land. During the 1834 cholera epidemic, two hundred and fifty people died in one single day. The coffins were left in porchways and under arches, then fetched at night. Funerals had to take place at once in the churchyards and the ringing of bells was prohibited.

In the nineteenth century, when Stockholm became an industrial city, the factories were usually situated on the islands. Fifteen thousand workers were occupied in the tobacco factories alone – women rolled the cigars and men made the snuff. Gustaf de Laval began to develop his separators and steam turbines in Kungsholmen. Alfred Nobel was experimenting with his explosive nitro-glycerine at Heleneborg in Södermalm, until his activities were prohibited in built-up areas as a consequence of an accident that claimed the lives of five people. Before the explosives factories were erected at Vinterviken, the substance was manufactured on a barge in Bocksundet at Ekerö.

The instrument firm of L.M. Ericsson sold telephones at Oxtorget. Sales were at first small and the apparatuses sold in pairs while no telephone network yet existed to link them to. But once the public network was developed during the 1880s, Stockholm was soon the city with more telephones than anywhere else in the world. A century later, the city repeated this record, this time with mobile phones.

Today a youth has swum far out in Riddarfjärden. He waves to a small group of gentlemen sitting on one of the smooth flat rocks of Långholmen, sharing a bottle of ice-cooled cheap wine. In the bay by

View from Södermalm towards City and Riddarholm Church ▷

Rålambshov's park, the stubby sternposts of sailing dinghies sweep close past each other. A multi-coloured kite hangs in the wind high up beneath the blue sky. The boy on the worn grass peers up at the sky and is dazzled by a reflection from a two-engined plane on its way to land at Bromma airport. On the edge of the water, children launch their armadas of wooden and plastic boats.

On the other side of Slussen where the waters of Lake Mälaren meet the waves of Saltsjön, some rowing-ladies at Räntmästartrappan call out their services. A wrinkled women is sitting there, wiping her sweaty forehead, her knees wide apart and her skirt pulled up over them. Her powerful shoulders can just be seen under her vest and her hair is dirty and lank. We get into her boat, thinking that in the afternoon, when over two hundred years have gone by, we can take the the Waxholm Company's ferry back.

The stifling heat is broken for a while by a quiet breeze from Saltsjön. The smell of sea and summer fills the gusts. There are boats moored all along the quays of Skeppsbron and Stadsgården. One last remaining surge from the wash of the Finland ferry that arrived this morning makes the rowing-boat lurch. The woman at the oars swears and brushes strands of hair from her forehead. A drop falls from her oar and the city expands in rings that extend over the water – year rings, rings of time, seasons.

Here, at what we nowadays call Blasieholmen, is where the man-of-war that was supposed to be the Crown's proudest ship was launched and equipped. One hot summer's day in 1628, perhaps a day like this when gusts of wind are the only cool in the hot August air, she set off on her maiden voyage, people waving and watching from along the quays and on the cliffs of Södermalm. The warship Vasa was a hundred metres or so out when a gust made the proud creation suddenly heel over and take fifty or so lives and sixty-eight guns into the depths with her.

Before we reach the jetties on Djurgården's shore, two more boats catch up with us. Singing is coming from one of them and in the prow lies a young woman dangling her hand in the wash round the keel, some of her friends waiting on the jetties below the inn at Gröna Lund. In the middle of the other boat next to ours is a man wiping his forehead, his wig on his lap, a youth in the stern holding his lute. Carl Michael Bellman is an elderly man, exhausted by the heat and longing for a nap in the shade of a tree. Nowadays he is only absently attracted by all the games he himself has described during outings to the inns of Djurgården.

The warship Vasa sank in Stockholm's harbour in 1628, but was rescued from the bottom of the sea in 1962. The ship is now one of the main sights of the city.

The fair sex settles their colourful troop on the heights out towards the edge of the water, some at Tegeludden, Biskopsudden, Blockhusudden and Fiskartorpet. The boys' manhood and shameless sabres attract but little their attention, so that one sister sighs, the next yawns and chews her sugar-bread, the third fingers her bib or nibbles at the feathers in her fan.

When the boats reach the jetty, Bellman laboriously gets up and stretches his limbs, perhaps thinking a few mouthfuls of wine would soon oil both body and mood, as he accepts the hand extended to help him up on to the jetty.

During the nineteenth century, Djurgården was turned into a landscaped park for the enjoyment of the aristocracy and the bourgeoisie. The rowdy life of pleasure of the eighteenth century became dainty and petty bourgeois, with tearooms and Swiss coffee-houses. On the first of May every year, the Court and Society made a habit of riding round Djurgården in carriages. Spectators crowded along Djurgården bridge as this moving cortege of the grand passed by on their first summer pleasure of the year.

Two hundred years after the little company from the boats has passed by, Gröna Lund is a playground with merry-go-rounds and attractions which none of them even dares, or wants to dream about. Blå Porten (the Blue Gateway) can just be seen further in among the trees, an inn previously called Lusthusporten (the Pleasure House Gate). This inn acquired its name from the little house built beside one of the gateways surrounding the royal hunting grounds. From her place in the house, Queen Kristina used to watch the animal-baiting between the trees. There was plenty of game in the grounds. King Karl XII was only seven when he took part in a hunt with nets for wolves in Djurgården.

There are animals all round the inn where the company before us are heading, hens galore and the cock is struggling with a worm that has no desire to leave its dark underworld. A speckled grey turkey struts by the garden gate where through a gap a shaggy dog quietly is mourning its captive life, surrounded by gnawed bones. About a century ago, there were still twelve hundred cows and seven hundred pigs in Stockholm, while today only a few can be seen in the enclosures in Skansen, where there is also an almost blind surviving wolf wandering its eternal way behind the wire netting.

Tilkänna gifves:
At
KONUNGENS TROTJENARE,
Hof-Secreteraren och Secreteraren
vid
Kongl. Numer-Lotterie Direction
Herr CARL MICH. BELLMAN
Med Döden afled
Den 11 Februarii 1795, klockan ett om natten, uti en
ålder af 54 år och 7 dagar.

Alla Sorgebesök undanbedes.

*No poet has sung the praises of Stockholm as Carl Michael Bellman
has. His songs deal mostly with a summer city, sun glittering on the
water, and drinking and lovemaking in alleys and leafy groves. Though
nor does he fight shy of the poverty of the city inhabitants, and at any
moment the cold shadow of death passes by uninvited. After being a wel-
come guest in the salons of the Stockholm bourgeoisie, he died burdened
by debt and illness after a spell in a debtors' prison. This is an announce-
ment of his funeral.*

*Riddarholmen with Storkyrkan (the Great
Church), Tyska kyrkan (the German Church),
and Riddarholm Church in the background* ▷

The company ahead stops by the outdoor inn that has been their goal. The aged Bellman has put his wig back on and sinks down on a chair in an arbour. They have already promised him a cooling glass of Rhine wine and spring-cold water, and the youth who has been carrying his lute asks whether we would not like to join them. But we continue on out towards Waldemarsudde, go to an exhibition, and then lie down on the grass. On the other side of the Saltsjö waters we can see an old cargo ship drawn up at Finnboda shipyard. Further in towards town, lunatics used to be put into Danviken's Asylum, where now terraced houses, tenements and oil storage tanks climb up the rocky slopes. White sails of sailing-boats flap in the wind, gulls hover on the summer breeze and at the edge of the water, a couple of ducks rest in the shade of a willow tree.

It is summer in Stockholm and we do not believe in that thing called autumn. Yet a cold shiver comes sweeping in over the water when an hour or two later we take the ferry back to Räntmästartrappan.

The sudden cold nips at our skin and we realize that we have dressed too carelessly for this day, which we obstinately wish to call summer. We take shelter when rain quietly starts falling. An exhausted man in dark damp clothes and a shaggy beard, coat of mail under his coat, stays on the after-deck.

A raindrop falls into the water, though the rings round it do not widen. The year closes and autumn requests us to begin all over again.

Sergels Torg (Sergel Square)

◁ *Riksdagen (the Parliament building)*

Detail from the Orpheus group by Carl Milles in front of Konserthuset (the Concert Hall)

Saturday trading in Drottninggatan

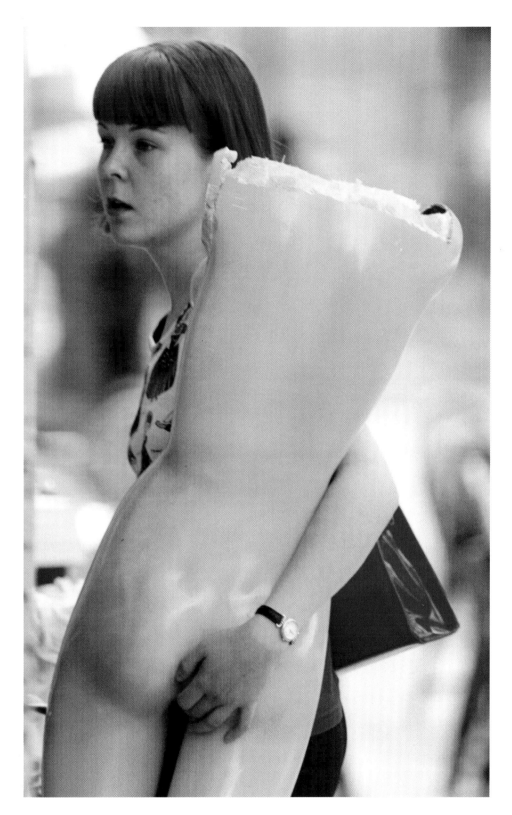

Stockholm is one the cities with the largest number of mobile phones in the world.

Most things can be found in the city's many shops.

Test of strength at the Water Festival climbing wall and summer gymnastics in Gärdet, Östermalm

A *new residential area has developed above the marshalling yard in Södermalm, dominated by this great building, called Bofills båge (Bofill's Arch), designed by the Spanish architect Ricardo Bofill.*

◁ *The Stockholm Marathon*

Rosenbad, the Sager House and the Royal Prince's Palace, government buildings in Norrmalm ▷

Summer and winter on Strömmen

White island boats link Stockholm with her archipelago, whose number of islands is one with the largest in the world. ▷

Today, Alfred Nobel is less remembered for his explosive inventions than for the prizes he established in his name. Every year, at one o'clock on an early October Thursday, the world press assembles outside the door of the permanent secretary of the Swedish Academy in the old Stock Exchange (Börshuset) to hear the name of the prize winner in literature.

◁ *Sailing Boat Day on Riddarfjärden*

Generations of figures in the world of theatre and film have worked at Dramatiska Teatern (the National Theatre) — Greta Garbo, Ingrid Bergman, Gösta Ekman, Ingmar Bergman, Max von Sydow…

Copies of two horses from St Mark's in Venice adorn Blasieholmstorg.

Early morning light over Moderna museet (Modern Museum) and Katarina Church.

The Water Festival attracts tourists from all over the world.

The Duck Race on Strömmen at the Water Festival

Summer is ending and the waters of Stockholm once again reflect the autumn colours.

◁ *Västerbron (the West Bridge) against one of the firework
displays on Riddarfjärden at the Water Festival*

COPYRIGHT ©1997 BY HANS HAMMARSKIÖLD (PHOTOGRAPHS)
AND NIKLAS RÅDSTRÖM (TEXT)
ORIGINAL TITLE: STOCKHOLM. DE FYRA ÅRSTIDERNA
GRAPHIC DESIGN BY BJÖRN BERGSTRÖM
TYPEFACE: ELECTRA 12/17
REPRODUCTION BY OFFSET-KOPIO, HELSINKI, FINLAND
PRINTED IN ITALY BY MILANOSTAMPA, FARIGLIANO, 1998
ISBN 91-46-17297-1

PICTURE ON PAGE 30: MARIABERGET, SÖDERMALM
PICTURE ON PAGE 60: JAKOB'S CHURCH IN KUNGSTRÄDGÅRDEN
PICTURE ON PAGE 88: TANTOLUNDEN ALLOTMENTS
AND HÖGALID CHURCH, SÖDERMALM